Let Gratitude Grow Your Faith

Copyright 2022 by Dachell Davis

All rights reserved. No part of this book may be reproduced, stored in a retrieval system, or transmitted in any form or by any means without the prior written permission of the publisher.

Cover Design: Double Chocolate Press

Printed in the United States of America

First Edition

Let Gratitude Grow Your Faith

DACHELL DAVIS

www.doublechocolatepress.com

**This book is dedicated to my children
and grandchildren:**

DeMarco, Ciera, Jeriah, Gabriel, Lelani, Braxton,
Lauryn and Devin – everything I do is for you!

Best Practices for Using this Daily Devotional:
The Let Gratitude Grow Your Faith

The Tears to Fearless Devotional Journal engages readers with a quick, meaningful connection to God each day. These devotionals will allow one the opportunity to reflect on His word, begin to focus more clearly on His will, and trust that His way is a perfect start or end to each day! The journaling page for each devotional provides space to record reflections on the readings and how it speaks to their spirit. In addition, the gratitude section furnishes a place to encourage each reader to immerse themselves in the good around them. And the prayer section allows space to record the reader's own petitions to God concerning anything that is on their heart!

Preface

Let Gratitude Grow Your Faith is the third book in my devotional journal book series. In case you are new to this series, *From Tears to Fearless* and *Finding Purpose Through Praise* are books one and two consecutively.

In this journal, you are encouraged to remember how gratitude can positively impact your daily living. Focusing more on the moment you are in and not what you are missing or still in need of, allows you to LIVE and not worry so much. Matthew 6:34 says, "Therefore, do not worry about tomorrow, for tomorrow will worry about itself. Each day has enough trouble of its own". React to your circumstances with thankfulness and watch how God will handle your troubles!

Through journaling, personal prayers and affirmations, you can use this book to connect with God in a meaningful and personal way. And that is a wonderful thing...

Dachell C. Davis
CEO/Author
Double Chocolate Press
www.doublechocolatepress.com

Let Gratitude Grow Your Faith

DACHELL DAVIS

"...Sing and make music from your heart to the Lord, always giving thanks to God the Father for everything, in the name of our Lord Jesus Christ"

(Ephesians 5:19, 20 NIV).

We all have SOMETHING to be thankful for. Simply waking up in the morning is a great way to begin your praise. God didn't have to do it, but He did! Praise Him for all that you have even when YOU don't think it's enough. Thank Him for all that you are, all that you have been through, and what there is still to come in your life. His blessings are continuous for those who live in obedience to His word! Sing Hallelujah to His precious and Holy name for He is truly GOOD!

_____

Date

Today's Affirmation

_____
_____
_____

Prayer and Reflection

_____
_____
_____
_____

Application

_____
_____
_____

Gratitude

_____
_____
_____
_____

Notes:

"Let them give thanks to the Lord for his unfailing love and his wonderful deeds for mankind, for he satisfies the thirsty and fills the hungry with good things"

(Psalm 107:8, 9 NIV).

When the Israelites were in the desert, they were literally dying of thirst and hunger because of their disobedience. They were stuck wandering around for 40 years. Most of you can head to the kitchen when you are hungry or thirsty, swing open pantry doors and refrigerators to choose from a plethora of options. Do you really take the time to realize how awesome that is? God loves you so much that He wants your life to be filled with abundance, provision, and daily reminders of His love! Take the time to thank Him for the sips of water you have readily available to you. It isn't so for many in the world RIGHT NOW. Do not take even the simplest things for granted, such as your morning coffee or tea...it is a BLESSING from God, not just a part of your daily routine that should be expected! This ease of life can be just as quickly taken away. So thank the Lord for His goodness, grace, and mercy...He is truly a WONDERFUL God!

_____

Date

Today's Affirmation

_____

_____

Prayer and Reflection

_____
_____
_____
_____

Application

_____
_____
_____
_____

Gratitude

_____
_____
_____
_____

Notes:

"Not to us, Lord, not to us but to your name be the glory, because of your love and faithfulness"

(Psalm 115:1 NIV).

Lord, today I thank you for my ability to worship, work, my family, friends, blessings seen and unseen! I give you all the glory, honor and praise because I was CHOSEN by you to see this day. Help me to rejoice and be thankful for all you have done, all you are doing right now, and all you have yet planned to do in my life. Let me enter into this day with your name on my lips and your spirit in my heart. I feel so amazingly blessed and fortunate because of YOUR love. I THANK YOU! In your precious and Holy Son Jesus' name...

_____
Date

Today's Affirmation

_____
_____
_____

Prayer and Reflection

_____
_____
_____
_____

Application

_____
_____
_____
_____

Gratitude

_____
_____
_____
_____

Notes:

"The Lord watches over the foreigner and sustains the fatherless and the widow, but he frustrates the ways of the wicked"

(Psalm 146:9 NIV).

Thank you, Lord, for providing love, protection, and care to those who are in need. You are magnificent in all your ways and your goodness cannot be compared! I can recall times where your hand covered and shielded me from the storm. You may not have stopped the winds from blowing, but You made sure that I did not get swept away. Continue to be my rock, my shield of protection, watching over me with Your attentive eye and comforting my hurt. Let my enemies fall before they can ever take hold of my life with the intention of ruin. Help me to always turn to you and be assured that You are there and You hear my prayers. In Jesus name…

_____

Date

Today's Affirmation

_____

_____

_____

Prayer and Reflection

_____

_____

_____

_____

Application

_____

_____

_____

_____

Gratitude

_____

_____

_____

_____

Notes:

"But, "Let the one who boasts boast in the Lord." For it is not the one who commends himself who is approved, but the one whom the Lord commends"

(2 Corinthians 10:17-18 NIV).

Everyone wants to receive credit for the work they have done. It's not necessarily a good feeling to work hard at something and someone else gets recognized for it, or the outcome itself is taken for granted. What you should realize is that the work you do should be done unto the glorification of the Lord, not man. He is the one who will reward good, honest, hard work. Whether you run a successful business or clean bathrooms for a living, do your work joyfully as if Christ himself is signing your paycheck. It is a blessing to even have a job. Thank God for His provision and do not worry about being recognized in praise for what you do. Your reward ultimately comes from the Father above and He is always excited to bless His children. Do your BEST work for God and receive the greatest acknowledgement you ever could—His grace, mercy, and favor... it is a wonderful thing!

_____
Date

Today's Affirmation
_____
_____
_____

Prayer and Reflection
_____
_____
_____
_____

Application
_____
_____
_____
_____

Gratitude
_____
_____
_____
_____

Notes:

"In the same way, the Spirit helps us in our weakness. We do not know what we ought to pray for, but the Spirit himself intercedes for us through wordless groans. And he who searches our hearts knows the mind of the Spirit, because the Spirit intercedes for God's people in accordance with the will of God"

(Romans 8:26, 27 NIV).

Thank you, Lord, for loving me SO MUCH that you are willing to decipher and decode my deepest indescribable thoughts and needs. It is amazing!

Do not think you have to go to God with pretty, eloquent prayers. Just open your heart and mind to Him and HE will search for what you cannot say. It's as simple as saying, "Lord, I need your help." Right then the Holy Spirit is on it, interceding for you and sharing with God exactly what you need. Thank God today that He appreciates a good mystery because many are lost and have such a deep desire to be found. As you enter into your prayer time, relax and know that all that is within you will be revealed (good and bad) according to what the Holy Spirit deems worthy. At minimum, pray God's will be done. That is really all you need. Pray, be still, listen, and receive God's blessings…it's a magnificent thing!

_____

Date

Today's Affirmation

_____

_____

_____

Prayer and Reflection

_____
_____
_____
_____

Application

_____
_____
_____
_____

Gratitude

_____
_____
_____
_____

Notes:

"Let the message of Christ dwell among you richly as you teach and admonish one another with all wisdom through psalms, hymns, and songs from the Spirit, singing to God with gratitude in your hearts. And whatever you do, whether in word or deed, do it all in the name of the Lord Jesus, giving thanks to God the Father through him"

(Colossians 3:16, 17 NIV).

No matter where you are or what you are doing today, take time to thank God for it all. He doesn't have to care for you the way that He does...BUT HE DOES! Be thankful for the most basic of things—waking up, seeing the beauty of creation, walking, talking, and thinking with your right mind. Tell somebody just how good God has been to you. Praise the Lord and absorb the goodness of His word. Whether in the church house or your own home, just WORSHIP HIM. Let your heart be filled with gratitude for every aspect of your being. Thank him for your family and friends, your job if you have one; your basic ability to live and love with a world full of possibilities each day. Thank you, Lord Jesus. Without you we would be lost!!

_____ Date

Today's Affirmation

_____
_____
_____

Prayer and Reflection

_____
_____
_____
_____

Application

_____
_____
_____

Gratitude

_____
_____
_____

Notes:

"For we do not have a high priest who is unable to empathize with our weaknesses, but we have one who has been tempted in every way, just as we are—yet he did not sin. Let us then approach God's throne of grace with confidence, so that we may receive mercy and find grace to help us in our time of need"

(Hebrews 4:15, 16 NIV).

Sin simply feels GOOD. Doing the things that we ought not to do generally brings some type of pleasure. How unfair is that? We have to fight temptation because it is the RIGHT thing to do, not because it makes us feel great to abstain from those desires. We all have weaknesses that we struggle with from time to time. Some as simple as an eating overindulgence - GLUTTONY. Yes, that is a sin! The Bible says in Proverbs 23:20–21 (ESV) "Be not among drunkards or among gluttonous eaters of meat, for the drunkard and the glutton will come to poverty, and slumber will clothe them with rags." But that ice cream sundae and extra helping of macaroni and cheese tastes so good! And, of course, you have to consider the obvious sins of lust, jealousy or anger. It's all about self-control. Pray the Lord gives you the same ability that Jesus had to resist. He felt what you feel, experienced pressures in life that should have caved His resolve, yet He NEVER gave in. You will never be perfect, but you can pray for enough of God's grace and mercy to get you through those moments. Tell the enemy "NOT TODAY!" Live in God's grace. Pray for His strength to defeat those calls to sin and be thankful that HE will always hear...it is a wonderful thing!

_____

Date

Today's Affirmation

_____

_____

_____

Prayer and Reflection

_____

_____

_____

_____

Application

_____

_____

_____

Gratitude

_____

_____

_____

Notes:

"When you have eaten and are satisfied, praise the Lord your God for the good land he has given you"

(Deuteronomy 8:10 NIV).

You can get so caught up in the joy of receiving a miraculous solution to your problems that you may forget to STOP and give thanks to the ultimate problem solver. When your cup runneth over and the blessings are in abundance, you often forget to settle down and continue to pray. You got what you needed, wanted, or desired, so all is right in your world. You tend to forget how it felt when you were in lack, hurting, or needing a great fix to your humongous problem. It is easy to do. Let's be real... when life feels amazing, praying can be difficult because you can get used to asking God for stuff but when you don't NEED anything, prayer must still be of utmost importance! Just like you appreciate a "thank you" when you have helped someone out, or given someone your time, attention or resources, God feels the same. He basks in your gratefulness. He then looks forward to blessing you AGAIN. Simply put, when you have prayed and God has answered your prayers, remember to THANK HIM. It is a necessary thing...

_____
Date

Today's Affirmation

_____
_____
_____

Prayer and Reflection

_____
_____
_____
_____

Application

_____
_____
_____

Gratitude

_____
_____
_____

Notes:

"God loved the world so much that he gave his one and only Son so that whoever believes in him may not be lost, but have eternal life"

(John 3 :16 NCV) .

Who can imagine a reason that one would have to sacrifice their child's life for another? Is there any EARTHLY reason you would willingly give up your own son or daughter for the greater good? Abraham was so faithful to God that He was on the verge of slaughtering his own son in obedience to Him. The concept is baffling! Yet that is exactly what God did to save your wretched soul. His reasons were HEAVENLY. He wants you close to Him, seeking Him, communing with Him always. And the manner in which He has insured that connection was through allowing His ONE and ONLY Son to die for you, thus opening the lines of communication with Him forever. He wants you to have eternal life through Jesus Christ. Pray to God in His Son's name and you WILL be heard. Why would you ever want to take that sacrifice for granted? Walk in the marvelous light of truth. Disregard the dark deeds of this world surrounding you and appreciate the gift of forgiveness Jesus so freely died for. Now THAT is an amazing thing...

_____
Date

Today's Affirmation

_____
_____
_____

Prayer and Reflection

_____
_____
_____
_____

Application

_____
_____
_____
_____

Gratitude

_____
_____
_____
_____

Notes:

"The God who made the world and everything in it is the Lord of heaven and earth and does not live in temples built by human hands. And he is not served by human hands, as if he needed anything. Rather, he himself gives everyone life and breath and everything else"

(Acts 17 :24-25 NIV) .

GRATEFULNESS...that is the word of the day. Think about all God has done for you. From the most basic (life, breath, health, strength) to the necessary (home, job, family, protection, provision) to the extraordinary (death, divorce, loss of physical and material things)...Be GRATEFUL for it all! Through each phase of your life you can learn to be who God desires you to be if you pay attention and take heed to the lessons. CHOOSE to listen, follow, and make adjustments where necessary. None of us is perfect, but we can choose to follow God who has ALL THINGS, needs NOTHING, and desires us to have EVERYTHING in His will. For in Him we live, move and have our being. Cherish the day. Share it with those you love and be encouraged to bless someone else in the day as well! That is a truly beautiful thing...

_____
Date

Today's Affirmation

_____
_____
_____

Prayer and Reflection

_____
_____
_____
_____

Application

_____
_____
_____
_____

Gratitude

_____
_____
_____
_____

Notes:

"...My grace is sufficient for you, for my power is made perfect in weakness." Therefore I will boast all the more gladly about my weaknesses, so that Christ's power may rest on me. That is why, for Christ's sake, I delight in weaknesses, in insults, in hardships, in persecutions, in difficulties. For when I am weak, then I am strong"

(2 Corinthians 12:9, 10 NIV).

We all go through times when we feel we have nothing left to give, we are all tapped out, tired beyond tired, we have had enough. BUT - how many times have you also felt that second wind? That final burst of strength, energy or confidence that got you through? These are the times when you should realize that it was by the GRACE of God and the power of the Holy Spirit that you made it! When you are down to your last, that is when God will show up and show just how magnificent He is. Therefore, still be joyful when all is NOT right in your world because you are bound to receive your spiritual, physical, mental or emotional boost. Our Father absolutely loves coming to our rescue when we trust Him for the solution to our problems. Put your boxing gloves down and pick up the best weapon you could ever use - the BIBLE! The power of His Word is sufficient for ALL our needs...

_____
Date

Today's Affirmation
_____
_____

Prayer and Reflection
_____
_____
_____
_____

Application
_____
_____
_____

Gratitude
_____
_____
_____

Notes:

"What shall I return to the Lord for all his goodness to me? I will lift up the cup of salvation and call on the name of the Lord"

(Psalm 116 :12-13 NIV) .

What do you typically do when someone does something nice for you? You say "thank you"...send them a card, email or text. Or take them out for a meal... repay the same kindness given to you. All of those things are wonderful. It is a blessing to be a blessing to others, so you should give thanks when a good hand is offered to you. But how do you thank someone who does not need anything? How do you repay the most amazing being in the world for all that He has done for you? What gift shop can you visit to accommodate the kind of thanks He would welcome? NONE. Because what God wants from you is you! He wants to hear His name cried out in love so He can answer you. "Praise the Lord, all you nations; extol him, all you peoples. For great is his love toward us, and the faithfulness of the Lord endures forever... (Psalm 117 :1-2 NIV). He wants to feel your prayers of gratitude and gratefulness so He can bless you. He wants you to live a life of godly character and peace. He wants you to bless others more than you sin for self. Sacrifice a bit of your time and attention and devote it to Him in prayer, praise, studying His Word, and fasting for clarity and understanding of His call on your life. Give Him the best you could ever give...your faith, love, hope, and belief in the power of His word! It is a FANTASTIC thing...

_____
Date

Today's Affirmation
_____
_____
_____

Prayer and Reflection
_____
_____
_____
_____

Application
_____
_____
_____
_____

Gratitude
_____
_____
_____
_____

Notes:

"But you are a chosen people, a royal priesthood, a holy nation, God's special possession, that you may declare the praises of him who called you out of darkness into his wonderful light"

(1 Peter 2 :9 NIV) .

How does it feel when someone selects you for a job or task that you had no idea you would even want to do? You hesitate, maybe try to think of an excuse to pass on the opportunity; work may be too hard; take too much time; you might not enjoy it. However, once you begin the work, you realize how rewarding it is. You're excited about how much you are learning, how your life is changing and improving because of the knowledge and experience you're gaining. You may even be getting a great big old paycheck for this work you thought was TOO HARD! That is how you should feel because you have been selected by God to be His chosen people. He calls you to live a holy life. That doesn't mean perfect; it means set apart from the rest. But that requires work, a conscious effort, and a desire to dig into the Word, gain its magnificent knowledge and practice its instruction in this harsh old world. Yes, it's hard sometimes. Sure, you may want to throw in the towel and give in to worldly desires from time to time, but because God has called you out of sinful darkness, you have to WANT to stay in the light of love, obedience, and faith. Put your hope and trust in your merciful God because He cares enough to save you from yourself. He urges us as His chosen children that He loves so very much, to live a GOOD life. We are His. There is no better relationship to be in than with your loving Father. That is an absolutely WONDERFUL thing...

_____

Date

Today's Affirmation

_____
_____
_____

Prayer and Reflection

_____
_____
_____
_____

Application

_____
_____
_____

Gratitude

_____
_____
_____

Notes:

"I will sing to the Lord all my life; I will sing praise to my God as long as I live. May my meditation be pleasing to him, as I rejoice in the Lord"

(Psalm 104 :33-34 NIV) .

What are you committed to? We all have something that we do or a way we behave that we rarely stray from. Whether it's a certain product we use, the way we dress, style our hair, clean our homes, interact with others, an attitude we present...there is a routine, process or habit that most of us follow each day that we don't change very much. Your commitment to Christ should be one of those things. You should be committed to praying, reading and studying the Word, praising and thanking God loudly and proudly. Let your heart be full of gratefulness and contentment regardless of your current circumstances. Your desire should be to please your Father BEFORE yourself. If you are lacking in any area of your relationship with God, make a renewed commitment to get it right. Do better and your blessings will BE better. It has to be a lifestyle, not a phase or a fall back plan. CHOOSE to praise and receive the power of the Holy Spirit. It is a wonderful thing...

_____
Date

Today's Affirmation

_____
_____

Prayer and Reflection

_____
_____
_____
_____

Application

_____
_____
_____
_____

Gratitude

_____
_____
_____
_____

Notes:

"This is what the Lord says: "Let not the wise boast of their wisdom or the strong boast of their strength or the rich boast of their riches, but let the one who boasts boast about this: that they have the understanding to know me, that I am the Lord, who exercises kindness, justice and righteousness on earth, for in these I delight," declares the Lord"

(Jeremiah 9 :23-24 NIV) .

We brag about many things in our lives. Our beautiful children, successful businesses, new cars and homes, great relationships with our significant others, but what do we gain from this? When you do it too much it can annoy others around you. If you do it with someone just as excited about what they have, you may end up in a competition of words about material gain. Trust me, God finds NOTHING delightful about boasting, unless it's about Him! There is so much more worth in giving your testimony about how good the Lord has been to you. Each day you awake with breath in your body and the ability to move about is enough right there. But many of you have so much more to brag on God about. How about when He rescued you from that abusive relationship? Or when you got a poor health report but all is well now in spite of it? Think about the time you lost your job but never missed a meal or a bill. Remember the difficulties you were having in your marriage or relationship, but now you two are more in love and committed than ever? Reminisce on the struggles you had raising your children alone but now they are thriving in college or leading productive adult lives. You were hurt so badly by someone you loved and trusted, but now your heart is healed and whole again. Tell somebody about those things. Be sure to give credit to your amazing Father in heaven for bringing you out, building you up again, and breaking down those barriers to your happiness and peace! He loves to hear His children talk about Him and share how gracious and loving He has been. Share your testimonies so another will be drawn to Him and desire to know how they can have the same goodness in their lives. Go ahead, tell someone your story. Make God smile...it is a beautiful thing!

_____
Date

Today's Affirmation

_____
_____
_____

Prayer and Reflection

_____
_____
_____
_____

Application

_____
_____
_____
_____

Gratitude

_____
_____
_____
_____

Notes:

"Joseph's master took him and put him in prison...But while Joseph was there in the prison, the Lord was with him; he showed him kindness and granted him favor in the eyes of the prison warden"

(Genesis 39 :20-21 NIV) .

Even when you are in what may be the worst position you have ever been in, it does not mean the Lord is not present. Have you ever been given a task or job to do that you were not happy about but still were successful? The person that placed you there expected you to suffer and fail, but instead you flourished! People around you noticed your skill and praised you. Eventually you were given more responsibility and were rewarded as well. While in the midst of a "prison" type of sentence, you were still being blessed! God shows favor to whomever HE wants, regardless of their position. His favor does not have to make sense. You could be demoted on your job to cleaning toilets one day and end up in charge of a whole custodial staff because of how well you polished those bowls. You have no idea what burdens God will transform into blessings at His will. Never believe that any work you put your hands to is too little or demeaning. God is able to make the last first. Be humble in your duties. Take charge of your dark periods. Let God know you trust Him in ALL of your circumstances. You may not love where you are right now, but know that God is with you. He will not allow your suffering to last too long; but just long enough for you to learn the lessons He needs you to learn. He cannot move you to the next level until you master the one you are on. Be gracious and grateful. Have a heart of humility and praise. You WILL get through this prison sentence and you WILL prosper. That is definitely something to look forward to.

_____
Date

Today's Affirmation

_____
_____
_____

Prayer and Reflection

_____
_____
_____
_____

Application

_____
_____
_____
_____

Gratitude

_____
_____
_____
_____

Notes:

"Yes, and the Lord will deliver me from every evil attack and will bring me safely into his heavenly Kingdom. All glory to God forever and ever! Amen"

(2 Timothy 4 :18 NLT).

I have begun the practice of saying I don't have bad days but moments within a day that aren't so great. If God was gracious enough to wake me with work for my hands, good intentions in my heart, and a shout of praise in my soul, the WHOLE DAY cannot be bad! But trust that evil has a way of trying that concept by being so busy that those difficult moments can add up to a whole lot of stress. This has been a week of mini attacks for me. From sleeping through my alarm and cutting back my devotional time one morning to getting locked out of my apartment on the weekend. I had little energy to work out this week, but lots of follow-through to cheat on my best intentions to eat right. My car would not start at the car wash after I gathered up the strength to vacuum it and wash it. Thank God for the gentlemen that were there to jump my car and wash it for free. My emotions have been high and tears threatened to fall on a few days, so I let them fall. But as I read this scripture today, I realized exactly who was walking with me through it all; how each and every battle ended up with a peaceful end. Even though evil was at many turns, I still smiled. While the enemy was attacking in random ways, I continued to thank God for His goodness. His desire is to see me through my trying moments, but it's up to me to focus on Him and not my inconveniences. Do not claim bad days but the goodness within each of those days! See the blessings as far greater than any of your burdens. Trust God for angels He sends when you are a bit overwhelmed. His presence, provision, and faithfulness are real for those who trust and believe in Him! Who do you trust for your deliverance?

Date

Today's Affirmation
_____
_____
_____

Prayer and Reflection
_____
_____
_____
_____

Application
_____
_____
_____
_____

Gratitude
_____
_____
_____
_____

Notes:

"...Who is this? He commands even the winds and the water, and they obey him"

(Luke 8 :25 NIV) .

Jesus is the commander of all of your storms. He can and will allow them to swoop in and wipe out some things while he can also immediately cease the winds and rain with one simple command. "...He got up and rebuked the wind and the raging waters; the storm subsided, and all was calm" (Luke 8:24 NIV). You must believe that if He permits certain catastrophes in your life, He can also order specific blessings to help you recover. You may not always come out on the other side of your storm with everything intact. Your hair may be a mess, a few things may have gotten soaked and ruined, and in some cases, there may be some things that drowned and did not make it out of the tsunami that nearly ripped your life apart. But what you have to be grateful for is the safety He brought you to afterwards, the shelter He ensured you had after the rain, the recovery of your sanity once the sun began to shine, the replacement of those objects or people that did not survive the connection to you during the storm. You are still standing after the divorce. Your health has returned after an unexpected illness. You are able to move on and start a new life after everything that was good and familiar to you was lost. Jesus is the designer of the bounce back life! You may get slammed against a wall, get passed around from heartache to heartache, hit your head on the concrete, but you will keep bouncing back to blessed when you keep your mind and spirit focused on Him! Hold steady to your faith even when full force winds are blowing and you are soaked to the bone with dire circumstances. You ARE coming out of this. ALL will be well again. Endure through prayer, meditation on the Word and perfectly placed hope in your Savior. THAT is the very best thing!

_____ Date

Today's Affirmation

_____
_____
_____

Prayer and Reflection

_____
_____
_____
_____

Application

_____
_____
_____
_____

Gratitude

_____
_____
_____
_____

Notes:

"Oh, the depth of the riches of the wisdom and knowledge of God! How unsearchable his judgments, and his paths beyond tracing out! "Who has known the mind of the Lord? Or who has been his counselor?" "Who has ever given to God, that God should repay them?" For from him and through him and for him are all things. To him be the glory forever! Amen"

(Romans 11 :33-36 NIV) .

God IS. There is no way you can fathom all that He is. He is IN everything, knows ALL things, and NEEDS nothing! There is not one thing that we could do to make Him indebted to us. We cannot be kind enough, love enough, or do enough good works that God would owe us anything. He is gracious, merciful, loving, and forgiving because He wants to be, not because we deserve it. We are naturally disobedient, sinful creatures as established in the Garden of Eden. But our Lord has always been of the heart to give us chance after chance to enter back into His good graces after a fall. Aren't you glad He never gives up on us like we try to do to Him when things do not go our way? Do not try to understand who He is, but be thankful and grateful that He IS... now that is a VERY good thing!

Date
_____

Today's Affirmation
_____
_____
_____

Prayer and Reflection
_____
_____
_____
_____

Application
_____
_____
_____
_____

Gratitude
_____
_____
_____
_____

Notes:

"For the Lord your God is God of gods and Lord of lords, the great God, mighty and awesome, who shows no partiality and accepts no bribes. He defends the cause of the fatherless and the widow, and loves the foreigner residing among you, giving them food and clothing"

(Deuteronomy 10 :17-18 NIV) .

Our God is a champion for the unfortunate, deprived, hopeless, and all who are in lack. He loves being the rock and provider whom we can depend. Even those who feel they have it all and need nothing should realize just WHO God is and has been for them. He is the King of kings, Lord of lords, Master of all the heavens and earth! No matter where you are in life, recognize that God is in the midst of your struggles as well as your successes. Never get too proud that you forget to give Him praise! He desires for you to walk in His ways, serve Him with all our heart and soul, and honor His command to love one another. "Fear the Lord your God and serve Him. Hold fast to Him and take your oaths in His name" (Deuteronomy 10:20 NIV). Desire to honor Him above all others and all things. He is GREAT. He is MIGHTY. He is WORTHY. Live, breathe and KNOW these things in your heart. It is a very good thing...

_____ Date

Today's Affirmation

_____
_____
_____

Prayer and Reflection

_____
_____
_____
_____

Application

_____
_____
_____

Gratitude

_____
_____
_____
_____

Notes:

"For you, Lord, have delivered me from death, my eyes from tears, my feet from stumbling, that I may walk before the Lord in the land of the living"

(Psalm 116 :8-9 NIV) .

Most of us have experienced instances of pain, hurt feelings, poor decisions, sinful behavior and a number of other things in this life that were not so pleasant. But because God loves you so much, you are still here. He gives you chance after chance to get life right and walk on the path of righteousness with Him. He has no desire to punish you for your faulty, flawed lifestyle and choices. What He wants is to draw you up and out of the pits you keep falling into and be given the glory for your rescue. He wants you to live a peaceful and joyful life right here on earth and be prepared to rest in heaven at your appointed time. There is no situation you are in that He cannot bring you out of and leave you standing in the light—the light of understanding and clarity about WHO He is and WHOSE you are. Do not give up and think things won't get better because God is gracious and full of compassion. (See Psalm 116:5). He is better to you than you could ever be to yourself! Be hopeful. Be vigilant in your prayers. Be mindful of His presence. Most of all, be thankful for His love, goodness, and generosity. He does not have to do what He does for you, but He chooses to.

_____

Date

Today's Affirmation

_____

_____

Prayer and Reflection

_____
_____
_____
_____

Application

_____
_____
_____
_____

Gratitude

_____
_____
_____
_____

Notes:

"Every good and perfect gift is from above, coming down from the Father of the heavenly lights, who does not change like shifting shadows"

(James 1 :17 NIV) .

Count your blessings! Take the time to literally take stock of the GOOD things in your life. Pick a day to carry a journal or notepad with you all day and make note of the positive gifts you see, feel, and hear. From the small things such as getting a good parking space at a busy store to something larger, such as thanking God for a particular healing of your body, mind, or spirit. Be excited about a wonderful tasting meal, a beautiful sunrise, a good cup of coffee/tea, or a great conversation with a friend. Praise God for your basic needs being met, such as shelter, clothing, food and the work you do. Count up all of the GOOD things you experience in the course of a day. Tell God how much you appreciate His love and provision and be grateful for each and every one of His blessings! You are so fortunate! It is imperative that you focus on the ways that are made for you instead of the opportunities you may have missed. Your heart should be joyful about the tiniest amount of favor that comes your way, as well as the supreme outpouring of God's goodness that many have been able to witness. Count up your gifts. Give God praise for them. Do not be afraid to show and tell others how GOOD He is!

_____
Date

Today's Affirmation

_____
_____

Prayer and Reflection

_____
_____
_____
_____

Application

_____
_____
_____
_____

Gratitude

_____
_____
_____
_____

Notes:

"For the foolishness of God is wiser than human wisdom, and the weakness of God is stronger than human strength"

(1 Corinthians 1 :25 NIV) .

The world has some extremely intelligent and strong individuals within it. The things that have been produced, created, concocted, initiated, and completed through great educated men and women are too numerous to name. Each and every day we are able to utilize many of these creature comforts. Then there is the physical strength that has been exhibited over and over by trained athletes, body-builders, and fitness fanatics all over the world. The weights are lifted, the balls bounced, thrown or kicked and the muscles are flexed. Yet none of these examples can compare to the wisdom, strength, and power of God! He is the reason all of these things are possible. On the worst day for God He is still greater, more powerful, and wiser than you and me. Many people think it is because of their hard work and determination that things get done, but what God provides for you in knowledge and capabilities is incomparable. You could never fathom it. The Lord says, "...the wisdom of the wise will perish, the intelligence of the intelligent will vanish" (Isaiah 29:14 NIV). With all that God knows and can do, you could never understand it. All you can and should do is be grateful and thankful for His extreme goodness and kindness to you and all of His amazing provisions! Do not take what you can do or the knowledge you have for granted. What God so freely gives He can just as easily take away. Boast in the Lord for He is simply THAT GOOD!

_____
Date

Today's Affirmation

_____
_____
_____

Prayer and Reflection

_____
_____
_____
_____

Application

_____
_____
_____
_____

Gratitude

_____
_____
_____
_____

Notes:

"All the days of the oppressed are wretched, but the cheerful heart has a continual feast"

(Proverbs 15 :15 NIV) .

How you live can be determined by how you ALLOW yourself to feel. You can have a meltdown about every little thing that goes wrong, or you can choose to accept the bad but exalt the good. Many people are down and depressed because they let the negative things of this world overpower the good. When you choose to focus on the blessings of your life instead of the burdens, life can be so much happier. Having a cheerful heart, pouring kindness out to those around you, and simply smiling even when you may be hurting, can bring the heart joy. God does not want you to suffer with depression and bad moods. He wants you to look at each day as an opportunity to do great things, love much, and serve without complaint. He wants you to live out your days spreading the good news of His Son Jesus and being the light that draws men and women to Him. There will be days when heartache is overwhelming and the pain and loss you have experienced seems to be too much, but those are the days when you MUST seek the Lord for your joy and not the world around you! Pray continually for the ability to see the good instead of the bad. Seek scriptures that help you to discern where God stands on the issues you may be dealing with. Cast your cares on the Lord and let Him be the source of your joy and strength. Love yourself enough to get up and do things that bring you happiness and be around people that make you feel good when your heart is not feeling so great. Make the choice to be cheerful. Feed your mind, body and spirit with GOOD things and watch the gloominess leave. Do not worry. Be happy...it is a good thing!

_____

Date

Today's Affirmation

_____

_____

Prayer and Reflection

_____
_____
_____
_____

Application

_____
_____
_____

Gratitude

_____
_____
_____
_____

Notes:

"But God said to Jonah, "Is it right for you to be angry about the plant?"...But the Lord said, "You have been concerned about this plant though you did not tend it or make it grow. It sprang up overnight and died overnight"

(Jonah 4 :9-10 NIV) .

We often take too much for granted. God blesses us, we are excited about it, but then we forget to do what needs to be done to maintain the blessing. As the scripture points out here, God gave Jonah a vine to provide shade and covering for him while he was out in the elements. It made Jonah more comfortable, but Jonah did nothing to ensure the vine stayed alive. As a living plant it needed care but Jonah neglected to care for the one thing that was covering and keeping him safe from the sun, so it died. How many times have you received a great blessing from God but you did not take care of it so you lost it? That relationship you were so excited about in the beginning, you got comfortable, your attention wandered, and you stopped doing what was needed to keep it alive and fresh so it ended. That new car you were able to buy with your bad credit - you drove it and did no preventive maintenance, so it broke down. That job you were so excited to have even though you did not meet all of the qualifications, yet you were hired anyway. You lost it because of poor attendance and frequent lateness to work. Learn to nurture your blessings even after you have received them. What the Lord gives He can just as easily take away. Be grateful for the things God has provided for you, especially those you did NOT deserve and never expected to have. He loves giving you the desires of your heart, so be gracious, thankful, humble, and keep working to maintain it. He didn't have to do it, but He did...and THAT is a wonderful thing!

_____

Date

Today's Affirmation

_____

_____

_____

Prayer and Reflection

_____
_____
_____
_____

Application

_____
_____
_____
_____

Gratitude

_____
_____
_____
_____

Notes:

"Because of the Lord's great love we are not consumed, for his compassions never fail" **(Lamentations 3 :22 NIV) .**

WHO is keeping you? This morning was not promised to any of us. As I sit here safe, secure, protected and provided for this morning, I want to impress upon you that today didn't have to come for me, for you, for any of us. The Lord CHOSE to keep us through the night. He CHOSE to open our eyes and give us the breath of life! In a blink of an eye, our lives can be changed. We could have NOT awakened this morning. DO NOT take this huge blessing for granted. This life is a gift, a blessing many can lose overnight. We should be THANKFUL for every moment, every life-giving breath. Everything we can see, touch, feel, hear and taste are ALL gifts from God. He chose to celebrate YOU today when you opened your eyes and your mind was sound, your body was healthy, you could move and walk and talk. Tell God THANK YOU. Ask God HOW He wants to use you today. Be ready and willing to serve him! This life is a blessing. THAT is a wonderful, marvelous, and amazing thing...

Date

Today's Affirmation

Prayer and Reflection

Application

Gratitude

Notes:

"Peace I leave with you; my peace I give you. I do not give to you as the world gives. Do not let your hearts be troubled and do not be afraid"

(John 14:27 NIV).

Do you accept it? This gift that was given to you is one that can only come from Him. This peace that surpasses understanding, that can guard your heart and mind, is precious and unfortunately rare for some. His desire is not to see you stressed, but blessed! Not worried, but encouraged! When you refuse to take your troubles to Jesus and carry them on your own, you ARE refusing the gift of peace. Children of God are not intended to be burdened, bogged down, or discouraged. You are to have peace regardless of your circumstances. No matter what you are going through, know that God is in control. Nothing is above His power. There is always the possibility of a second chance. A do-over. Do NOT fear starting over again. His peace will be what keeps you sane in this crazy old world. Jesus left His peace with you as He returned to His heavenly home to keep you until He comes again. Cherish it, embrace it, and leave the worries of the world to Him. Now that is a special thing...

_____
Date

Today's Affirmation

_____

_____

_____

Prayer and Reflection

_____
_____
_____
_____

Application

_____
_____
_____
_____

Gratitude

_____
_____
_____
_____

Notes:

"They were amazed at his teaching, because his words had authority"

(Luke 4:32 NIV).

Have you been captured yet? Has the word of God, the commands of His Son Jesus, gotten your attention? It is amazing what the Word of God can do. It has opened many an eye about how to live, love, and BE. When the Word of God wraps itself around you and takes hold of your soul, you will be in awe of its miraculous power. At His command, Jesus cast out demons, healed the sick, raised the dead, fed the hungry, and saved wretched souls. Lives are changed when Christ enters the picture. He wants you to recognize His works, big and small. He wants you to be grateful for the simple things as well as the major breakthroughs you have experienced in your life. Jesus has the ability to make a way out of no way. He can open doors no man can shut. His power can change the biggest sinner into the most grateful saint! Recognize His awesome grace and mercy. Be changed by the lessons that His word teaches. Believe that your prayers in His name have the power to cause special and exciting things to happen. Praise Him for all He has done and continues to do in your life. BE AMAZED...it is a wonderful thing!

_____
Date

Today's Affirmation

_____
_____
_____

Prayer and Reflection

_____
_____
_____
_____

Application

_____
_____
_____
_____

Gratitude

_____
_____
_____
_____

Notes:

"Do everything without grumbling or arguing, so that you may become blameless and pure, "children of God without fault in a warped and crooked generation." Then you will shine among them like stars in the sky"

(Philippians 2:14-15 NIV).

Complain much? Are you more in tune to what is wrong in your life or what is right? Complaining introduces an opportunity for more issues. It can open the door to discontent and can become a breeding ground for disappointment and unhappiness. Once you begin to focus on the bad things around you, you are no longer living with an attitude of gratitude. You should be thankful for ALL of the wonderful things God is doing in your life instead of zooming in on what is less than perfect. Society has become so used to getting things now, working less to get them, and always looking for the upgrade. People are not satisfied with life as it is. Contentment lasts only for a moment as boredom sets in and you begin to want more. Scriptures say you are to be without fault in a warped and crooked generation! You are to show thanksgiving for what has been, what is right now and what will be in your future at the hand of God. Look for the GREAT in your circumstances! Take your focus off of what you still don't have and tell God *thank you* for what you do have. In time the desires of your heart, what you are praying for, will come to pass if it is the will of God. He has been too GOOD for you not to be GRATEFUL. That is a GREAT thing...

_____

Date

Today's Affirmation

_____

_____

Prayer and Reflection

_____
_____
_____
_____

Application

_____
_____
_____

Gratitude

_____
_____
_____
_____

Notes:

"Look at the birds of the air; they do not sow or reap or store away in barns, and yet your heavenly Father feeds them. Are you not much more valuable than they?"

(Matthew 6:26 NIV).

You really are! There is nothing God would like more than to ensure your most basic needs are met. He does not want you to want for anything that you need. His love is so great for you that He even wants you to have some of your heart's desires as well. Your desires should also fall in line with His will. All of us are not meant to have mansions, fancy cars, and fat bank accounts. Many of us tend to want to declare our personal greatness when we get too much. Take the credit. Leave God in the background. And in the end, those are the people who truly aren't all that happy. Having MUCH does not have to mean having things. You can be wealthy with love, in compassion, with great relationships, and purposeful work. Do not get too caught up in the idea of things you think you should have to be happy. Gratefulness should be expressed for the simplest things. The air you breathe, food you eat, shelter, and clothes you have to wear. God has promised to provide these things and does not want you to question it. You mean that much to Him! You are VALUABLE. You are WORTHY. You are his child and He loves you so very much. And in order to have all that you need you must first seek after God. "But seek first his kingdom and his righteousness, and all these things will be given to you as well" (Matthew 6:33 NIV). Get in His Word, praise Him for all He has done and continues to do. Be content in your right now, and be prepared for what's next. He has it for you. All you have to do is GO GET IT! THAT is a wonderful thing...

_____ Date

Today's Affirmation

_____
_____

Prayer and Reflection

_____
_____
_____
_____

Application

_____
_____
_____

Gratitude

_____
_____
_____

Notes:

"...and provide for those who grieve in Zion— to bestow on them a crown of beauty instead of ashes, the oil of joy instead of mourning, and a garment of praise instead of a spirit of despair. They will be called oaks of righteousness, a planting of the Lord for the display of his splendor"

(Isaiah 61:3 NIV).

"Recovering from pain or disappointment of any kind is not something that just happens to some people and not to others. It is a decision! You make a decision to let go and move on. You learn from your mistakes. You gather up the fragments of your life and give them to Jesus, and He will make sure that nothing is wasted (see John 6:12). You refuse to think about what you have lost; instead, you inventory what you have left and begin using it with a thankful heart."

~Joyce Meyer

You can still have beauty from your ashes. You can get back all that the enemy has stolen. You can be WHOLE again. Trust God with the pieces of your life that have been broken. He can and He will turn them into something beautiful if YOU let Him. Make the choice to be grateful. Decide that you will survive. Have a greater desire to WIN than you do to WALLOW in your pain. Give it to Jesus...it will be the BEST thing you have ever done. His healing is an amazing thing...

_____
Date

Today's Affirmation
_____
_____
_____

Prayer and Reflection
_____
_____
_____
_____

Application
_____
_____
_____
_____

Gratitude
_____
_____
_____
_____

Notes:

ABOUT THE AUTHOR

Dachell Davis is a native of Dayton, Ohio. She attended Trotwood Madison High School and graduated from Colonel White High School. She attended Southwestern College of Business shortly after graduation, majoring in Business Administration. Later in life she also attended the University of Phoenix and The Art Institute of Pittsburgh studying Business Management and Fashion and Retail Management, respectively.

Dachell loves being creative and was a passionate sewer for many years. She enjoyed making clothing for her children and herself on occasion. Dachell's first small business was a children's clothing and accessory company which she ended up closing in 2019.

Currently her favorite hobby is decorative planning. Pen to paper is the most fulfilling way for her to plan her days!

While being an avid reader all her life, writing has always been something that came naturally to her. After sharing her devotional messages via social media for many years, Dachell was urged by the

Holy Spirit to begin telling her story and from there her first book, *From Tears to Fearless* was born.

Most recently, Dachell worked in Human Resources before transitioning her career to pursue her entrepreneurial dreams in 2022. She is currently the CEO/Founder of Double Chocolate Press, where she works as an author, inspirational coach and creator of many other beautiful and functional items.

As a great lover of coffee, Dachell will also have uniquely flavored coffee available on her website in January 2023 – *What's in Your Cup – Café Blends*. Her goal is to open a coffee shop and bookstore to meld two of her greatest passions together in the very near future.

Stay connected with Dachell by visiting www.doublechocolatepress.com.

You can also connect with her on social media platforms:

IG: @dachelldavis and @designing_my_days
Facebook: @dachelldavis
Twitter: @dachell_davis
TikTok: @dachelldavis

Thank you!

My biggest thank you always is to God for leading my way on this publishing journey. There are many days when I wonder if what I am doing is making a difference, and He quickly reminds me that His word will never return void and shall accomplish His will (see Isaiah 55:11). He has promised to never leave me to figure things out alone and I know this to be true. His blessings and favor show up each time I go through this process so I will keep going until He says I am done!

Additionally, I am so grateful for the love and support from my partner in life, *James H. McCray*. Your love and support are invaluable. So much of what I do right now, is because of your belief in me and my dreams. Thank you so much!

And finally, I thank YOU, my readers, for being a part of my dreams by purchasing, reading and gifting my books. The messages written herein are directly from God through me and designed to show you who HE is. I pray that each message has brought you a little closer to His love for you. None of what I do would be possible without your support.

Double Chocolate Press
w w w . d o u b l e c h o c o l a t e p r e s s . c o m

Made in the USA
Monee, IL
30 April 2024

57722142R00118